# "FOUR GOLDEN KEYS"

# "FOUR GOLDEN KEYS"

## Unlocking the Key Verses in the Gospels

TIMOTHY CROSS

## Ambassador International
### GREENVILLE, SOUTH CAROLINA & BELFAST, NORTHERN IRELAND

www.ambassador-international.com

# Four Golden Keys

Unlocking the Key Verses in the Gospels

ISBN: 978-1-935507-50-5

Printed by Bethel Solutions

Ambassador International
Emerald House
427 Wade Hampton Blvd
Greenville, SC 29609, USA

Ambassador Books and Media
The Mount
2 Woodstock Link
Belfast, BT6 8DD, Northern Ireland, UK

www.ambassador-international.com

# CONTENTS

# INTRODUCTION

*A river flowed out of Eden to water the garden, and there it divided and became four rivers* (Genesis 2:10).

The Apostle John ended his Gospel by saying that the life of Christ was so awesome, and the things He did so amazing, that were every one of them to be written, I suppose that the world itself could not contain the books that would be written (John 21:25).

The Holy Spirit of God however has seen fit to bequeath us four written accounts of the life and ministry of the Lord Jesus Christ. He did this through His servants Matthew, Mark, Luke and John - men who were divinely prepared for a divinely prepared task. Apart from these four Gospels, our historical knowledge of the life, death and resurrection of the Son of God would be negligible. These four Gospels thus repay our careful and prayerful reading and re-reading like no other literature.

Interestingly, each Gospel writer has his own particular stress and perspective on the same Person of Christ. If four artists were to paint your portrait, it would be the same 'you' portrayed on each of the four canvases. Yet each painting, paradoxically, would be different, as each painter would have a different perspective and style. Likewise with the four Gospels. The same Christ is portrayed by all four writers, yet each one has his own particular slant:-

i. Matthew emphasises that Jesus is the Messiah, the King of the Jews, the fulfilment of all the Old Testament longings, hopes and prophecies.

ii. Mark emphasises that Jesus is the Servant of God, Who came to lay down His life to ransom sinners.

iii. Luke emphasises that Jesus is the compassionate Son of Man Who came to save sinners

iv. John emphasises that Jesus is the eternal Son of God, through Whom we may come to know eternal life.

The four Gospels take up a large proportion of space in the New Testament. Matthew has twenty eight chapters; Mark has sixteen chapters, Luke has twenty four chapters and John has twenty one chapters. At first, this may seem a little overwhelming. We cannot see the wood for the trees! But take heart. Each Gospel writer has given us a key to unlock the whole of his Gospel - a clue verse or verses which unlock all the chapters he has written.

The following four chapters are entitled *Four Golden Keys.* They focus on the key verses of each of the four Gospels - verses which when grasped and understood will give us an understanding of the whole. Just as a house has a specific key which lets us enter in and explore all of its rooms, the key verses of the Gospels we are about to study will let us into each of the Gospels, unlocking the door to allow us in on all of their chapters and the peculiar blessing of the Christ related therein the Christ Who is Himself the Gospel. My prayer and hope is that as you read the following pages, your mind will be enlightened, your heart warmed, and your appreciation of and your devotion to the Christ of the Gospel will be increased.

The pages which follow began life as a mini series of evening sermons also entitled *Four Golden Keys.* They were preached at the Saltmead Presbyterian Church, Grangetown, Cardiff, during the autumn/winter of 2009. I am very grateful to those who listened to the sermons with such interest and attention, and encouraged me to write them up with a view to sharing them with a wider audience. Christian fellowship is a foretaste of heaven itself. To the tri-une God be all the glory.

**Timothy Cross**

# BEHOLD YOUR KING
## THE GOLDEN KEY TO MATTHEW'S GOSPEL

*This took place to fulfil what was spoken by the prophet, say-*
*ing, 'Tell the daughter of Zion, Behold your king is coming to you,*
*humble and mounted on an ass, and on a colt the foal of an ass'*
(Matthew 21:4,5).

These verses here in Matthew 21:4,5 are key verses. These two verses, in fact, give us the key to unlock all twenty eight chapters of Matthew's Gospel.

Each Gospel has its own particular slant and perspective on the Lord Jesus Christ. Matthew's particular perspective is that Jesus is the longed for Messiah. Matthew directs our attention to the King of the Jews. *Behold your king is coming to you …* The Lord Jesus' kingship is one facet of His being the Messiah, for as the Messiah, He combines the three-fold offices of prophet, priest and king in His One Person.

Matthew's Gospel is the most Jewish in 'flavour' of all of the four Gospels. Matthew stresses that Jesus is the fulfillment of the prophecies and promises God had made in the Old Testament Scriptures. Matthew - of course - is the first book in our New Testament. Showing, as he does, how Jesus is the fulfillment of the Old Testament hopes and longings, Matthew is thus the ideal bridge between the two testaments. He completes what the Old Testament commences.

Matthew directs us to the longed for Messiah. *Behold your king.* Unusually though, he points us to a crucified king. At the Cross

11

of Calvary he noted carefully that *over His head they put the charge against Him which read, 'This is Jesus the king of the Jews'* (Matthew 27:37).

Let us now look a little more closely at 'the golden keys of Matthew's Gospel' - verses which unlock the whole of Matthew's book, and let us in to the reality of God's Christ:-

*This* (that is, the events of 'Palm Sunday') *took place to fulfil what was spoken by the prophet, saying 'Tell the daughter of Zion, Behold your king is coming to you, humble and mounted on an ass, and on a colt the foal of an ass.'* The verses direct our attention to the Scriptures of God, the Saints of God and the Sovereign of God. We can consider them under the three headings of:-

1. The Prophecy God Spoke

2. The People God Selected

3. The Prince God Sent

**1. The Prophecy God Spoke**

*This took place to fulfil what was spoken by the prophet ...*

Some four hundred years before the events of Palm Sunday, the prophet Zechariah had prophesied that the Messiah would enter Jerusalem as He did. Zechariah - or rather, God through Zechariah - foretold the details of the day which has become known as 'Palm Sunday.' Zechariah 9:9 reads *Lo, your king comes to you; triumphant and victorious is He, humble and riding on an ass, on a colt the foal of an ass.* Those around in Zechariah's day must have been puzzled. A humble Monarch seems to be a contradiction. A God on a donkey seems totally farfetched. All though became clear in its fulfillment in Christ.

The events of Palm Sunday remind us that there was nothing random, haphazard or accidental about the birth, life, death and resurrection of the Lord Jesus Christ. All was in accord with what God had foretold in the Scriptures. The fulfillment of Scripture is actually one of the evidences that the Bible is the Word of God. God alone knows the end from the beginning, so God alone can foretell history in advance. Palm Sunday then was all part of God's eternal plan of redemption. It set into motion the events which were to result in Christ's procuring the redemption of His people by His death on Calvary's cross. The hymn writer wrote:-

Ride on ride on in majesty!

In lowly pomp ride on to die

O Christ, Thy triumphs now begin

O'er captive death and conquered sin.

Almighty God has His eternal plan of redemption - a plan to save for Himself a people of His Own for His Own glory. At the dawn of history, He promised in Genesis 3:15 that the seed of the woman would eventually come and bruise the serpent's head - that is, come and undo the ravages which sin had wrought. God put His eternal plan into effect in time. In the fullness of time, this Redeemer came, just as God had promised. *But when the time had fully come, God sent forth His Son, born of woman, born under the law, to redeem those who were under the law* (Galatians 4:4).

The coming of Christ then - as Matthew points out - was all according to the Scriptures. God fulfils His prophecies. God keeps His promises. We have reason to trust God's Word. We have every reason to have confidence in Almighty God. Nothing can thwart Him. Nothing can frustrate His plans. He is in sovereign control of the universe as the one *Who accomplishes all things according to the counsel of His will* (Ephesians 1:11). Nothing could, would or can undo or undermine God's eternal plan of redemption, focused and centered on His Son. *This took place to fulfil what was spoken by the prophet ...*

*I know that Thou canst do all things and that no purpose of Thine can be thwarted* (Job 42:2)

*The LORD of hosts has sworn: 'As I have planned, so shall it be, and as I have purposed, so shall it stand'* (Isaiah 14:24)

*I work and who can hinder it?* (Isaiah 43:13).

Note the prophecy God spoke.

## 2. The People God Selected

*Tell the daughter of Zion, Behold your king ...*

We have reference here to a particular people, namely, *the daughter of Zion.* The Bible is clear that Christ came for both a specific purpose and for a specific people. He came to redeem God's elect, both Jew and non Jew. These people, says Paul, are, in the eternal plan of God, chosen in Christ *before the foundation of the world* (Ephesians 1:3).

Matthew 1:21 reads *You shall call His name Jesus for He will save His people from their sins.* So we see that Christ came to save a specific people - those foreordained and predestined by God for eternal salvation. These people - the blessed of the blessed - are referred to by various names in the Bible: They are the saved, the redeemed, the elect, the saints ... Here they are referred to as *the daughter of Zion.* Paul refers to them as *the Israel of God* (Galatians 6:16) and it is these people who constitute the true church of God - the community of the redeemed. Ephesians 5:25 explains how *Christ loved the church and gave Himself up for her that He might sanctify her, having cleansed her by the washing of water with the word.* Peter wrote to some scattered Christians reminding them that *you are a chosen race, a royal priesthood, a holy nation, God's Own people ...* (1 Peter 2:9).

How though can we know whether we belong to the true people of God - those chosen by God for eternal salvation? If we belong to Jesus, we may be sure that we are numbered among God's elect, for those predestined by God in eternity past will be effectually drawn to Christ in time, and enabled to trust Him for eternal salvation. Romans 8:30 asserts: *those whom He predestined He also called; and those whom He called He also justified; and those whom He justified He also glorified.*

So God has His chosen people. Thank God that nothing can hinder the salvation of God's elect - those whom Christ came to save. Jesus said in Matthew 16:16: *'I will build My church, and the powers of death shall not prevail against it.'*

Note then the people whom God selected. *Tell the daughter of Zion, Behold your king ...* It is these people - the 'children of Zion' - who are the 'dearest and the blessed' and, whatever their lot in this world, do not wish to exchange places with anyone else in all the universe:-

Saviour, since of Zion's city

I through grace a member am

Let the world deride or pity

I will glory in Thy Name

Fading is the worldling's pleasure

All his boasted pomp and show

Solid joys and lasting treasure

None but Zion's children know.

Matthew's Gospel though is pre-eminently the Gospel of King Jesus. Hence the 'golden key' of his Gospel points us distinctly to:-

## 3. The Prince God Sent

*Behold, your king is coming to you, humble and mounted on an ass, and on a colt the foal of an ass.*

Behold, your King! The Prince God sent. We are reminded here from both the verses and their context of Jesus' Sovereignty, Deity and Humility.

### i. The Sovereignty of the Prince God Sent

*Behold, your king* ... 'Hail to the Lord's anointed, great David's Greater Son!' Jesus is the King of kings - His kingship being one facet of His being the Messiah. The ass was actually a royal animal of Jewish kings. In 1 Kings 1:32 we read *And the king (David) said to them 'Take with you the servants of your Lord, and cause Solomon my son to ride on my own mule ... let Zadok ... and Nathan ... anoint him king over Israel.* Hence, on 'Palm Sunday', Jesus was, accordingly, given royal acclaim. They *spread their garments on the road, and others cut branches from the trees and spread them on the road ... (they) shouted 'Hosanna to the Son of David! ...'* (Matthew 21:8,9). This was the way in which kings were treated and acclaimed in Old Testament times. 2 Kings 9:13 relates how *in haste every man took his garment and put it under him on the bare steps and they blew the trumpet and proclaimed 'Jehu is king.'*

The Christian's loyalty and allegiance is to King Jesus. The Christian contends 'For Christ's crown and covenant.' Jesus is the King of kings and Lord of lords. God says of Him *I have set My King on Zion, my holy hill* (Psalm 2:6). The *Shorter Catechism* explains:-

> Christ executeth the office of a king in subduing us to Himself, in ruling and defending us, and in restraining and conquering all His and our enemies.

Christians worship an enthroned Christ, seated at the right hand of God *far above all rule and authority and power and dominion and above every name that is named, not only in this age but also in that which is to come; and He has put all things under His feet and has made Him the head over all things for the church* (Ephesians 1:21,22).

Christians worship an unrivalled King and also worship a coming King. Paradoxically, Jesus reigns and Jesus is coming to reign. The events of Palm Sunday seem to give us a foreshadowing of the events of the Last Day, if we have eyes to see. With prophetic foresight, Revelation 19:11 describes the Second Coming of Christ so:-

*Then I saw heaven opened, and behold, a white horse! He Who sat upon it is called Faithful and True, and in righteousness He judges and makes war ... On His robe and on His thigh He has a name inscribed, King of kings and Lord of lords.* Note the sovereignty of the Prince God sent. Note also:-

## ii. The Deity of the Prince God Sent

There is evidence of Christ's deity in the incident of Palm Sunday. Remember that in dealing with Christ we are dealing with God in the flesh. Mark's Gospel tells us that the colt on which Jesus rode was one *on which no one has ever sat* (Mark 11:2), that is, - to be technical - the colt had not been 'broken in.' The question then is begged: Why did the colt not bolt? Why did the colt accept its Rider and not get agitated - especially when we consider the surrounding crowd, with its noise, agitation and excitement? The answer is: Because the Creator was riding it. The One with total dominion was riding the ass, and the mute creature recognised its Creator and submitted to Him.

It is written of Christ in Psalm 8:6 ff. that *Thou hast given Him dominion over the works of Thy hands; Thou hast put all things under His feet, all sheep and oxen, and also the beasts of the field.* So Christ was in total control of this mute, wild animal - a 'beast of the field.' Such reveals that Jesus Christ is God. Scripture everywhere reveals His deity. Who but God could calm the story sea, heal the sick, raise the dead, forgive sins and bestow eternal life. Sovereignty and deity characterise the Christ Who rode into Jerusalem on a lowly ass - as did humility:-

### iii. The Humility of the Prince God Sent

*Behold your king is coming to you, humble and mounted on an ass* ...This King, unusually, is characterised by both majesty and meekness. The horse is an animal of war, but the humble ass is an animal of peace. Jesus is the *Prince of Peace* (Isaiah 9:6). He was actually on a peace mission - riding to Calvary to make peace between God and man. Colossians 1:20 explains His *making peace by the blood of His cross.*

The ass is a beast of burden - and Jesus was going to Calvary to bear the burden of our sin, for *He Himself bore our sins in His body on the tree* (1 Peter 2:24). The ass is a working animal, and the Lord Jesus had a specific work to do. *The Son of Man came not to be served but to serve and to give His life as a ransom for many* (Mark 10:45). The Lord Jesus was riding into Jerusalem to accomplish a work - the work of redemption. Christians rest on and rejoice in the finished Work of Christ at Calvary: the One sacrifice which Christ made - the sacrifice of Himself - the sacrifice which alone is able to save eternally those who put their faith in the crucified Christ.

*Behold your king is coming to you, humble ...* This seems to encapsulate the whole life and ministry of the Saviour. He stooped to conquer. He became poor so that we could know the riches of eternal salvation. He humbled Himself in time so that by His humiliating death on the cross, we could be eternally exalted:-

*Have this mind among yourselves which is yours in Christ Jesus, Who though He was in the form of God did not count equality with God a thing to be grasped, but emptied Himself, taking the form of a servant, being born in the likeness of men. And being found in human form He humbled Himself and became obedient unto death, even death on a cross ...* (Philippians 2:5 ff.).

So the Lord Jesus humbled Himself. He rode into Jerusalem to great acclaim. But He was on a mission. He was riding to Calvary to procure the eternal salvation of all who put their faith in Him.

The key verses of Matthew's Gospel then - in-line with all of his Gospel - direct us to our Redeemer-King. The Lord Jesus is the Anointed One of God. He was sent - as promised in the Scriptures - to accomplish the redemption of God's people. *This took place to fulfil what was spoken by the prophet, saying, 'Tell the daughter of Zion, Behold your king is coming to you, humble and mounted on an ass, and on a colt, the foal of an ass.'* Our response to this can only be to bow before Him and say:-

All glory, laud and honour
To Thee Redeemer-King


Thou art the King of Israel
Thou David's royal Son
Who in the Lord's Name comest
The King and blessed One


To Thee before Thy passion
They sang their hymns of praise
To Thee now high exalted
Our melody we raise


All glory, laud and honour
To Thee Redeemer-King
To Whom the lips of children
Made sweet hosannas ring.

# THE SUPERLATIVE SERVANT-SAVIOUR
# THE GOLDEN KEY TO MARK'S GOSPEL

*For the Son of Man came not to be served but to serve, and to give His life as a ransom for many* (Mark 10:45).

Mark 10:45 is *the* key verse which unlocks every verse of Mark's sixteen chaptered account of the Gospel of our Lord and Saviour Jesus Christ. Mark's particular portrait of the Lord Jesus is that of the Servant. In Mark 1-10 he describes how this superlative Servant-Saviour gave His life in service; and in Mark 11-16, he describes how the superlative Servant-Saviour gave His life in sacrifice - a sacrifice to ransom many; a sacrifice which saves God's people for time and eternity.

In Mark 10:45 then we have a most important verse. It is the clue verse of Mark's Gospel, and it is one of the earliest explicit statements as to the exact purpose of Christ's coming into the world: He came to serve, and He came to lay down His life to ransom our souls. The verse is crystal clear, and whilst written down by Mark under the inspiration of the Holy Spirit, we note also that it originally came from the very lips of the Servant-Saviour Himself. Here we are given His Own understanding of His life, ministry and death - an understanding we will do well to read, ponder and heed. Harold Paisley says of Mark 10:45:-

> This verse is the greatest and most significant in this Gospel. It its two clauses it forms the key to the whole ministry of the perfect Servant. The

first clause covers the first ten chapters of this Gospel 'For the Son of Man came not to be ministered unto but to minister'; and the last clause 'to give His life a ransom for many' covers the last chapters, eleven to sixteen. The Lord of glory had veiled His glory and come into the world as God's perfect Servant (Philippians 2:6-8). His service was climaxed in His death as a ransom for many. His death was voluntary, violent, vicarious and victorious.

Analysing this defining verse in Mark 10:45 a little more closely, we note four points:-

1. The Significant Title - *the Son of Man*

2. The Special Travels - *came*

3.. The Specific Task - *to serve*

4.. The Saving Truth - *to give His life as a ransom for many.*

## 1. THE SIGNIFICANT TITLE

*For the Son of Man …*

Our Lord's preferred way of referring to Himself was by using this designation: 'the Son of Man.' It is a significant title. Paradoxically, it both conceals and reveals His true identity. In using this title, we are taught both the humanity and the deity of our Saviour.

i. His Humanity

*The Son of Man …* The 'Son of Man' is a human title. In Ezekiel 2:1 the LORD God spoke to Ezekiel so: *'Son of man, stand upon your feet, and I will speak with you.'* The title reminds us that our Lord was a real Man. He shared our humanity, sin apart. *The Word became flesh and dwelt among us, full of grace and truth* (John

1:14). The Son of God became a Son of Man that the sons of men might become the sons of God.

> Christ the Son of God became Man by taking to Himself a true body and a reasonable soul, being conceived by the power of the Holy Ghost in the womb of the virgin Mary and born of her, yet without sin (*Shorter Catechism*).

In Christ, we have a sympathetic Saviour. He knows what it is like to be human, as He became a *Son of Man.* He was born, humanly, into a large, poor family, who all lived under one roof in a one roomed housed in first century Israel. He experienced hunger and thirst. He knew fatigue. He experienced the frustrations of the workaday. He knew the slander of His enemies and hurtful betrayal of His friends. On the cross, He experienced the most excruciating physical, psychological and spiritual pains. John 11:35 informs us how *Jesus wept.* He did so because He shared our physical, psychological and emotional frame.

The significant title *The Son of Man* then reminds us of our Saviour's humanity. We have a sympathetic Saviour Who has 'walked in our shoes.' *We have not a high priest Who is unable to sympathise with our weaknesses, but one Who in every respect has been tempted as we are, yet without sin* (Hebrews 4:15):-


Does Jesus care when my heart is pained
Too deeply for mirth or song?
As the burdens press
And the cares distress
And the day grows weary and long?

O yes, He cares, I know He cares
His heart is touched with my grief
When the days are weary, the long nights dreary
I know my Saviour cares.

In Christ, God became Man. The title *the Son of Man* reveals His true humanity.

ii. His Deity

The title *Son of Man* reveals Christ's humanity, but also conceals His deity - or conceals it if we do not know the full biblical significance of the term.

Daniel 7:13,14 clearly shows that in dealing with the Son of Man we are dealing with One Who is no less than God. Daniel 7:13,14 reads *I saw in the night visions, and behold, with the clouds of heaven there came One like a SON OF MAN, and He came to the Ancient of Days and was presented to Him. And to Him was given dominion and glory and kingdom, that all peoples, nations and languages should serve Him; His dominion is an everlasting dominion, which shall never pass away, and His kingdom one that shall not be destroyed.*

Here then we are dealing with deity. 'Thou art the king of glory O Christ, Thou art the everlasting Son of the Father.' To Jesus belongs dominion, glory, kingdom and authority. His dominion is an everlasting dominion. His kingdom is one that shall not be destroyed. At the name of Jesus, every knee shall bow!

*The son of man.* It is a significant title, as it reveals both the humanity and deity of our Saviour. As a man, He could die. As the God-man, His death alone could ransom our souls. His death alone is a sacrifice which atones for sin and saves eternally.


**2. THE SPECIAL TRAVELS**

*The Son of Man also came* ...

Here we glimpse the special travels of the Son of Man. He made the greatest journey of all. He left heaven for earth, that we might leave earth for heaven. No foreign missionary journey can ever compare with the journey made by the Lord Jesus Christ. His was the ultimate in cross-cultural mission. He left the glory of heaven, to enter this sin-scarred world, so that we who are sinners might be saved by His grace, and enter the glories of the mansions above. He was born so that we might be born again. He entered into time so that we might be saved for eternity. He became poor so that we might become rich. He, the sinless One, came to earth to be made sin for us, so that we, the sinful ones, might be reckoned righteous in God's sight, and rendered fit for heaven.

*The Son of Man also <u>came</u>* ... Note His special travels:-

Thou didst leave Thy throne
And Thy kingly crown
When Thou cams to earth for me ...

Thou camest O Lord
With the living Word
That should set Thy people free
But with mocking scorn
And with crown of thorn
They bore Thee to Calvary

O come to my heart Lord Jesus
Thy cross is my only plea.

The reference to Christ's 'coming' here gives us a glimpse of Christ's pre-existence. Bethlehem marked His birth, but not His beginning. Christ existed before He was born. He existed eternally. Eternity is an attribute of God - so we see again the deity of our Lord Jesus Christ. He is the eternal Son of God, the second Person of the Trinity.

In Psalm 90:2 it is written of God: *From everlasting to everlasting Thou art God.* God has no beginning or end. He is the great

'I AM.' Christ too had no beginning. We glimpse this here when He mentions His coming into the world on His ministerial mercy mission from heaven. *The Son of Man ... came ...* We also glimpse this when we tread on the holy ground and read the so called 'high priestly prayer' which Christ prayed to His Father before His impending death. There He prayed *'Father, glorify Thou Me in Thy Own presence with the glory which I had with Thee before the world was made'* (John 17:5).

*The Son of Man ... came.* No such thing could be said in the biography of even the greatest human being of this world. Christ is the pre-existent One. He is God. He always was - but He came into the world to save sinners. The eternal One alone was able to offer an eternal sacrifice. He came!:-

*Christ Jesus came into the world to save sinners* (1 Timothy 1:15).

*When the time had fully come, God sent forth His Son, born of woman, born under the law, to redeem those who were under the law ...* (Galatians 4:4 ff.).

So we note the special travels of the Son of God and Son of Man. In Jesus, the eternal entered into time. *In the beginning was the Word ... the Word became flesh and dwelt among us ...* (John 1:1,14):-

But none of the ransomed ever knew

How deep were the waters crossed

Nor how dark was the night that the Lord passed through

Ere He found His sheep that was lost

He came from the brightest of glory

His blood as a ransom He gave

To purchase eternal redemption

And Oh He is mighty to save!

## 3. THE SPECIFIC TASK

*For the Son of Man came not to be served but to serve, and to give
His life as a ransom for many* (Mark 10:45).

Service and sacrifice then were the Saviour's Own 'job de-
scription' and the reason why He came to this earth: He came to live
His life as a Servant, and He came to give His life as a sacrifice - *as
a ransom for many.*

We note first of all that Christ came *to serve.* Centuries pre-
viously, God had foretold through His servant, the prophet Isaiah,
that this would be so. In Isaiah 42:1 God had said: *Behold, My Servant, Whom I uphold, My chosen in Whom My soul delights; I have
put my Spirit upon Him ...*

Then, in what is believed to be an early Christian hymn,
and creedal statement, we read Paul's words in Philippians 2:5-7:
*Have this mind among yourselves, which is yours in Christ Jesus,
Who, though He was in the form of God did not count equality with
God a thing to be grasped, but emptied Himself, taking the form of a
<u>servant,</u> being born in the likeness of men.* This summarises much
of what we have considered about Mark 10:45 so far.

The context of Mark 10:45 makes Christ's statement stand
out starkly. James and John - and by implication, all the disciples -
had just asked the Saviour that He would bestow on them a place
of eminence in glory. They asked Jesus *'Grant us to sit, one at your
right hand and one at your left, in your glory'* (Mark 10:37). They
sought 'to be served.' They, as have millions since, had a lust for
'power and glory.' The Saviour however turned their thinking upside
down. He said that the way up is the way down - that the way to
true greatness is the way of lowly service. This lowly service was
exemplified supremely in His Own life, ministry and ultimately in the
sacrifice of Himself at Calvary. Jesus certainly 'practised what He
preached.' In John 13 we can read of His taking on the role of the
lowest of household slaves, when He *laid aside His garments, and
girded Himself with a towel. Then He poured water into a basin, and*

*began to wash the disciples' feet, and to wipe them with the towel with which He was girded* (John 13:4,5).

This is our God, the Servant-King

He calls us now to follow Him.

*The Son of Man came not to be served but to serve ...* In eternity past, Christ was certainly served, for He dwelt in the harmony of the Trinity, in the mutual love and unity of the Father and the Holy Spirit. At the present time and for all eternity, Christ is and will be served. 1 Peter 3:22 informs us that Christ *has gone into heaven and is at the right hand of God, with angels authorities and powers subject to Him.* The redeemed in heaven *serve Him day and night within His temple* (Revelation 7:15). Christ is and is to be served, as He is God. But when He came to earth, He came *not to be served but to serve ...*

This brings us to one of the basic tenets of the Christian Faith, and it is this: Christianity is not what we do for God, but what He in Christ does for us. The Christian Faith is concerned, primarily, with Christ's service for us, and not our service for Him. According to the Bible, we are saved by Christ's work for us, received by faith, and not our own supposed meritorious works which we do for Him. 'Churchianity' though, and nominal Christianity always puts the stress on what we do, and not on what Christ has done. The message of the Bible though is that 'Salvation is of the Lord.' If we are to be of service for Christ, how vital it is that we are first of all served by Christ and saved by Christ. A basic fundamental of the Christian Faith is that our salvation is all of grace, and our service is all of gratitude. Yet how many millions in Christendom are confused here and believe implicitly or explicitly that salvation is by our human efforts and endeavors? The Bible is clear; we are saved solely by the work of God in Christ on the cross - His supreme service for us. *By grace you have been saved through faith and this is not your own doing it is the gift of God not because of works lest any man should boast* (Ephesians 2:8,9).

Note then the specific task which Christ came to fulfil. He came to live His life as a Servant - *not to be served but to serve* - and

He came to give His life as a sacrifice. This leads us to our last and vital point:-

## 4. THE SAVING TRUTH

*The Son of Man also came not to be served but to serve and to give His life as a ransom for many* (Mark 10:45).

*… to give His life as a ransom for many.* This brings us to the saving truth, for it brings us to the cross of Calvary, where Christ, the Good Shepherd, laid down His life for the sheep.

In chapter ten of Mark's Gospel, we are brought fact to face with both a telling prophecy of Calvary and the true purpose of Calvary. The reality of Christ's cross comes into focus, and the reason for it as well. Look at Christ's detailed prophecy concerning His impending crucifixion in Mark 10:32 ff.:-

*And they were on the road, going up to Jerusalem, and Jesus was walking ahead of them; and they were amazed, and those who followed were afraid. And taking the twelve again, He began to tell them what was to happen to Him saying 'Behold, we are going up to Jerusalem, and the Son of Man will be delivered to the chief priests and the scribes, and they will condemn Him to death, and deliver Him to the Gentiles; and they will mock Him, and spit upon Him, and scourge Him, and kill Him; and after three days He will rise.'*

Note the reality of Calvary - Christ prophesied it. But note also the reason for Calvary. It was to be *a ransom for many.* A ransom! There was point and purpose to Christ's death. And we come now to the central and saving truth of the Christian Faith. Nothing could be more basic. The theme runs right through the New Testament:-

*There is one God and there is one Mediator between God and men the Man Christ Jesus Who gave Himself as a <u>ransom </u>for all* (1 Timothy 2:5).

*You know that you were <u>ransomed</u> from the futile ways in-*

herited from you fathers, not with perishable things such as silver or gold, but with the precious blood of Christ, like that of a lamb without blemish or spot* (1 Peter 1:18,19).

*Thou wast slain and by Thy blood didst <u>ransom</u> men for God* (Revelation 5:9).

*... a ransom for many.* To what was the Lord Jesus referring here?

## A Ransom

A ransom is a payment. To ransom means to set free by paying a ransom price. New Testament times were characterised by slavery. A slave was in bondage to his master for life. It was possible though to buy your freedom - to buy yourself out of slavery - if you could save up enough money, or if a kindly benefactor had pity on you and paid for your freedom himself.

To ransom means to deliver by paying a price. A ransom is a payment made to set another free. Sin has put us into God's debt. Sin has put us in bondage to divine condemnation. But Christ is the great debt payer and liberator from condemnation. The GOSPEL proclaims that God's Own Son Paid Every Liability:-

There was no other good enough

To pay the price of sin

He only could unlock the gate

Of heaven and let us in.

On Calvary's cross Christ paid the ransom price for our release. He gave His life to free us from the penalty we deserve for our sins. He died to deliver us from condemnation, enduring the wrath of God on our sins to free us from the wrath of God for our sins. Sin has a price and a penalty. All sin is ultimately against God, and sin has to be paid for. On the cross, Christ paid the price for us. His death was *a ransom for many.* The word 'for' is the Greek word 'anti'. It means 'in the place of, instead of, on behalf of.' Satisfaction by substitution takes us to the heart of the meaning of Calvary. *Christ died for our sins* (1 Corinthians 15:3). 'He gave His life to ransom my soul.'

In closing, we purport that Mark 10:45 has an evangelistic application. In the light of eternity and the coming of Christ, the question is begged: Do you know the one who can clear all your debts against a holy God? Do you know the Saviour-Servant Who can ransom your soul and save you for all eternity? Can you say, from the heart: Yes. I am a sinner, I am in God's debt, I deserve eternal condemnation, but:-

> Jesus paid it all
> Paid it on the tree
> I could never pay the debt
> But Jesus died for me.

> He upon Calvary, He, upon Calvary
> An offering for sinners became
> He paid the debt of sin
> That forgiveness might flow in
> Unto all who believe in His name.

Mark 10:45 then is the golden key which unlocks all the chapters of Mark's Gospel. Mark focuses our attention on the superlative, Servant-Saviour. *The Son of Man also came not to be served but to give His life as a ransom for many.*

# THE COMPASSIONATE SAVIOUR OF SINNERS
## THE GOLDEN KEY TO LUKE'S GOSPEL

*For the Son of Man came to seek and to save the lost* (Luke 19:10).

Our verse here in Luke 19:10 contains words from the Lord Jesus' very own lips. With this statement, the incident of Zacchaeus the tax collector's saving encounter with Christ is brought to a climax and conclusion.

Luke 19:10 is the golden key which unlocks all twenty four chapters of Luke's Gospel, and even a golden key to unlock the whole of the Bible. The theme of Luke's Gospel is the Saviour and His great salvation - and the message of the whole Bible may also be summarised under the heading 'The Saviour and His Great Salvation' :-

*For God sent the Son into the world, not to condemn the world, but that the world might be saved through Him* (John 3:17).

*Christ Jesus came into the world to save sinners* (1 Timothy 1:15).

*We have seen and testify that the Father has sent His Son as the Saviour of the world* (1 John 4:14).

Each Gospel writer - Matthew, Mark, Luke and John - has his own particular slant, angle, stress and emphasis on the one Person of Christ. Luke's particular perspective is that Jesus is the Saviour of sinners. *This man receives sinners and eats with them* (Luke 15:2). *The Son of Man came to seek and to save the lost* (Luke 19:10).

*Luke the beloved physician* (Colossians 4:14) portrays Jesus as the compassionate Son of Man, eternal in His deity yet real and tender in His humanity. His reason for leaving heaven for earth - says our verse - was a rescue mission: He came to save sinners from a lost eternity in hell, and procure for them a place in God's glorious heaven.

No one would seriously deny that the Lord Jesus existed at all. We prove His reality with our calendar each day - His coming into the world has divided time into the eras of BC and AD. But the exact reason for Christ's coming into the world is debated and disputed. Opinion and speculation vary. Some view Him as just a great teacher. Others consider Him as a moral reformer, or even a revolutionary … But how did Christ Himself view His mission? Luke 19:10 tells us. *The Son of Man came to seek and to save the lost.* Casting off and aside all human opinion and speculation then, let us put Luke 19:10 under a magnifying glass and consider the Saviour's own explanation for His coming into the world. We may divide the verse into four:-

1. The Christ: The Designation of Jesus

2. The Coming: The Descent of Jesus

3. The Condition: The Diagnosis of Jesus

4. The Cross: The Deliverance of Jesus

**1. The Christ: The Designation of Jesus**

*The Son of Man came to seek and to save the lost* (Luke 19:10).

The self-designation of 'The Son of Man' is a title that the Lord Jesus applied to Himself and described of Himself more frequently than any other. Christ is 'the Son of Man.' It has been well said that 'the Son of God became a Son of Man, that the sons of men might become the sons of God.' The title 'Son of Man' is a loaded one. It conceals both the tender humanity and the absolute deity of the Lord Jesus Christ.

### i. His Tender Humanity

God, in Christ, became a man - the 'Son of Man.' He shared our flesh and blood. He knows what it is like to be human, sin apart. In Christ we have a Saviour who knows. He knows all about our human condition. He knows all about our trials and tribulations, pains and perplexities, as He has been through them, and suffered them Himself. No remote deity have we here! He is the compassionate Son of Man, infinite in sympathy:-

*The Word became flesh and dwelt among us ...* (John 1:14).

*Since therefore the children share in flesh and blood, He Himself likewise partook of the same nature* (Hebrews 2:14).

*For we have not a high priest Who is unable to sympathise with our weaknesses, but One Who in every respect has been tempted as we are, yet without sin* (Hebrews 4:15).

The designation 'Son of Man' then reveals the Lord Jesus to be a Saviour or real humanity and utmost sympathy:-

Though now ascended up on high
He bends on earth a brother's eye
Partaker of the human name
He knows the frailty of our frame

Our fellow-sufferer yet retains
A fellow-feeling of our pains
And still remembers in the skies
His tears, His agonies and cries

In every pang that rends the heart
The Man of Sorrows had a part
He sympathises with our grief
And to the sufferer sends relief.

The designation 'Son of Man' reveals Christ's tender humanity, but it also conceals:-

## ii. His Absolute Deity

This 'Son of Man' is awesome and incomparable. He is God. He is the Second Person of the Trinity. Every knee shall bow to Him one day, as universal dominion belongs to Him.

The title 'Son of Man' is not as modest as you might think at first. The title is taken from the book of Daniel, where it is there used of the Sovereign of the universe:-

*Behold, with the clouds of heaven there came one like a son of man, and He came to the Ancient of Days and was presented before Him. And to Him was given dominion and glory and kingdom, that all peoples, nations and languages should serve Him; His dominion is an everlasting dominion which shall not pass away, and His kingdom one that shall not be destroyed* (Daniel 7:13,14).

Claiming to be the 'Son of Man' is actually a claim to deity. Using the designation of oneself would be blasphemy were it not true. We see this from the trial of the Lord Jesus before the high priest. On trial, and under oath, the Lord Jesus told the high priest *'You will see the Son of Man seated at the right hand of Power and coming with the clouds of heaven.'* The reaction? *And the high priest tore his garments, and said 'Why do we still need witnesses? You have heard His blasphemy ...'* (Mark 14:62:ff.).

Christians thus contend for both the tender humanity and the absolute deity of the Lord Jesus Christ. He is a Friend, for sure, but also God. He is the God-man, ever to be worshipped and adored. He alone is worthy. Christians confess gladly to committing Christolatry. The Lord Jesus Christ is incomparable. John, in his vision, saw:-

*In the midst of the lampstands one like a son of man ... His voice was like the sound of many waters ... from His mouth issued a sharp two-edged sword, and His face was like the sun shining in full strength. When I saw Him, I fell at His feet as though dead ...* (Revelation 1:13 ff.).

Reverence then becomes the Lord Jesus Christ. Every knee shall bow to this 'Son of Man.'

## 2. The Coming: The Descent of Jesus

*The Son of Man* <u>*came*</u> ...

Luke 19:10 implies the Saviour's pre-existence. For Jesus to come, He had to exist already. Scripture testifies to the fact that Christ did exist already. He existed eternally in the divine fellowship of the divine trinity of Father, Son and Holy Spirit. He is the eternal Son of God. There never was a time when He was not!

John opens His Gospel explaining that *In the beginning was the Word and the Word was with God and the Word was God* (John 1:1). In John 17:5 Jesus spoke to His Father of *the glory which I had with Thee before the world was made.*

*The Son of Man* <u>*came*</u> ...He came from the brightest of glory. 'Thou didst leave Thy throne and Thy kingly crown, when thou camest to earth for me ...' The Son of Man left heaven for earth, so that the sons of men might leave earth for heaven. 'For us men and for our salvation He came down from heaven.' He was born so that we might be born again. 'He came from His blest throne, salvation to bestow.' He descended to earth so that sinners might ascend to heaven, saved by His grace. He became poor, so that poverty stricken sinners might know the eternal riches of His salvation. *You know the grace of our Lord Jesus Christ, that though He was rich, yet for your sake He became poor, so that by His poverty you might become rich* (2 Corinthians 8:9).

The Coming: The Descent of Jesus. It was the greatest missionary journey ever made - unsurpassed and unsurpassable. He came on a rescue mission for *the Son of Man came to seek and to save the lost.* He came to procure the salvation of God's elect by dying in their place at Calvary, and so paying the penalty for their sin. He came!:-

Thou Who was rich beyond all splendour

All for love's sake becamest poor

Thrones for a manger didst surrender

Sapphire-paved courts for stable floor

Thou Who was rich beyond all splendour

All for love's sake becamest poor


Thou Who art God beyond all praising

All for love's sake becamest man

Stooping so low, but sinners raising

Heavenwards by Thine eternal plan

Thou Who art God beyond all praising

All for love's sake becamest man.


## 3. The Condition: The Diagnosis of Jesus

*For the Son of Man came to seek and to save the lost.*

According to the Lord Jesus - and according to the whole Bible - our condition, by nature, is a sad one. In fact, it is a deplorable one, even a damnable one. We are *lost.* And apart from the grace of God in Christ, we will be lost eternally, in hell. Lost! It's a sad and sorry word. The diagnosis though always precedes the cure. Dr Luke the physician who recorded Jesus' words would have been well aware of that. By nature, we are lost in our sin. *Behold, I was brought forth in iniquity, and in sin did my mother conceive me* (Psalm 51:5).

Isaiah 53:6 tells us that *All we like sheep have gone astray; we have turned everyone to his own way.* We have turned away from God, and in doing so have lost our way. Our sin separates us from God our Maker, and renders us liable to His wrath. Our sin puts us in peril. Our sin makes us *lost.* Scripture is crystal clear: *None is righteous, no, not one; no one understands, no one seeks for God. All have turned aside, together they have gone wrong …* (Romans 3:10 ff.).

In Luke 19:10, the clue verse to Luke's Gospel, the Lord Jesus is teaching that we are lost and need to be found. In Luke 15 we can read three parables from the lips of the Saviour. The three parables concern three lost things which were eventually found. Luke 15 contains the parables of a lost sheep, some lost silver and a lost son. The parables are illustrative both of our lost condition and the consequent joy which accompanies being found or saved. We are like lost sheep, we have wandered away from God. We are like a lost coin - hopeless and helpless to save ourselves. We are like that rebellious son and in need of repentance - turning back to God. We need to be saved from our sin. We need a Saviour. And Jesus is the Saviour for our need, for the Gospel proclaims: *The Son of Man came to seek and to save the lost.*

Luke 19:10 is a statement the Lord Jesus made just after he had sought out and saved lost Zacchaeus, a somewhat crooked tax collector. The Good News is that the Lord Jesus still seeks out and saves lost sinners, even today, and bestows on them His eternal salvation. He is a Saviour who really saves. He saves the lost. Jesus is the only hope for this lost, condemned world.

Note carefully then our lost condition - the diagnosis which Jesus made and still makes of us. Matthew Henry comments on Luke's golden key:-

> Observe the deplorable case of the sons of men: they were *lost*; and here the whole race of mankind is spoken of as one body. Note, the whole of mankind, by the fall, is become a lost world: lost as a city is lost when it has revolted to the rebels, as a traveller is lost when he has missed his way in the wilderness, as a sick man is lost when his disease is incurable, or a prisoner is lost when sentence is passed upon him.

*Lost.* We need to be saved. Conviction precedes conversion - and only the Holy Spirit of God can bring this about. The diagnosis precedes the cure. A recognition of the malady always precedes seeking the correct remedy. The Bible alone diagnosis the correct condition of the human soul. It is cruel to be kind. It does not flatter us. We are sinners who need a Saviour. Christ alone is the answer to our deepest need. He alone can save, and save eternally! Which leads us to:-

## 4. The Cross: The Deliverance of Jesus

The Christian Church has a Gospel to proclaim. Why? *For the Son of Man came to seek and to save the lost* (Luke 19:10). Christ saves because He gave His life as a sinless, soul-saving, atoning sacrifice at Calvary. And by His Holy Spirit, He still seeks out sinners, and draws them effectually to Himself, enabling them to receive all the soul-saving benefits of the saving sacrifice He once made:-

> Effectual calling is the work of God's Spirit whereby convincing us of our sin and misery, enlightening our minds in the knowledge of God and renewing our wills, He doth persuade and enable us to embrace Jesus Christ, freely offered to us in the Gospel (*Shorter Catechism*).

The Christ of the Bible is a seeking and a saving Saviour. In fact, the God of the Bible is a God Who seeks and saves sinners. Way back at the dawn of history, when our first ancestors had sinned and brought on themselves and us our lost condition, God sought them out and saved them by His grace. *The LORD God called to the man and said to him 'Where are you?'* (Genesis 3:9). And in His mercy He clothed them, thus covering their sin and shame. He literally provided a sacrifice of atonement for them.

### Context

In the Bible, context is very important in understanding any particular verse. The words of Luke 19:10 were spoken by the Lord Jesus just after He had saved Zacchaeus, and as He approached His impending cross.

The cross is integral to God's eternal plan of salvation to save a people for Himself. The Lord Jesus knew this, so *taking the twelve, He said to them, 'Behold, we are going up to Jerusalem, and everything that is written of the Son of Man by the prophets will be accomplished. For He will be delivered to the Gentiles, and will be mocked and shamefully treated and spit upon; they will scourge Him and kill him, and on the third day He will rise'* (Luke 18:31 ff.). When the Lord Jesus spoke Luke 19:10 then, He was journeying to Jerusalem with the sole purpose of dying on a cross to procure the eternal salvation of God's elect.

The Cross: the deliverance of Jesus. Salvation was procured by the Christ Who died at Calvary for all who believe - that is, avail themselves of His saving death. At Calvary, Christ died in the place of sinners. At Calvary He bore the wrath of God due to sinners. At Calvary, Christ Himself momentarily became lost! He experienced the outer darkness of hell. He was separated from His Father so that we might be eternally reconciled to the Father. He suffered so we might be saved. He was lost so that we might be found. He was forsaken so that we might be forgiven. Scripture is crystal clear:-

*You shall call His name Jesus for He will save His people from their sins* (Matthew 1:21)

*He was put to death for our trespasses ...* (Romans 4:25)

*Christ died for the ungodly* (Romans 5:6)

*Christ died for our sins in accordance with the Scriptures* (1 Corinthians 15:3)

*For the Son of Man came to seek and to save the lost* (Luke 19:10).

Scripture is adamant that there is no other Saviour and there is no other Gospel. Luke was to record later *there is salvation in no one else, for there is no other name under heaven, given among men, by which we must be saved* (Acts 4:12). Here is the Gospel to proclaim. Here is a Gospel to embrace. Here is a salvation to celebrate. Jesus saves! The golden key which unlocks Luke's Gospel tells us unequivocally: *the Son of Man came to seek and to save the lost* (Luke 19:10).

41

Whoever receiveth the crucified One
Whoever believeth on God's only son
A free and a perfect salvation shall have
For He is abundantly able to save

Whoever receiveth the message of God
And trusts in the power of the soul-cleansing blood
A full and eternal redemption shall have
For He is both able and willing to save.

# THE INCOMPARABLE SON OF GOD
# THE GOLDEN KEY TO JOHN'S GOSPEL

*But these are written that you may believe that Jesus is the Christ,
the Son of God, and that believing you may have life in His name*
(John 20:31).

John 20:31 is the key and clue verse to the whole of the Apostle John's twenty one chaptered account of the life and ministry and death and resurrection of the Lord Jesus Christ. John was completely open and 'above board.' He had no hidden agenda. He was honest, and confessed that - under God - he intended his Gospel record to be used as propaganda for the Christian Faith. The purpose behind his Gospel was both evangelical and evangelistic.

If we were to take John - *the beloved disciple* - aside for a moment, we could ask him: 'John. Why did you write your account of the works, words and ways of the Lord Jesus Whom you followed so closely for those amazing three years of your life? What motivated you to take up your pen?' John would surely reply. 'Let me tell you. Here's my Gospel. And this was *written that you may believe that Jesus is the Christ, the Son of God, and that believing you may have life in His name.*'

Here then in John 20:31 we have the key which unlocks the whole of the Gospel of John. And here also - it is not going too far to state - is a key to unlock the whole Bible. The whole Bible was written to bring us to faith - saving faith - in Christ. The Bible was written so that we may know and enjoy the greatest blessing of all, namely *the free gift of God (which) is eternal life in Christ Jesus our Lord* (Romans 6:23).

Notice from John 20:31 that the Bible and Christ are insepa- rable. The Bible brings us to faith in Christ and the Bible confirms and strengthens our faith in Christ - until that day, when faith will give place to sight, and we will have no further need for the Bible, for we will be in the presence of the Christ of the Bible for all eternity. We will only be able to dispense with the written Word when we are in the immediate presence of the living Word. Until that day, those of us who know the incarnate Word are beholden to and in glad bondage to the inspired Word.

So let us examine John 20:31 a little more closely. It is one of the most significant and important verses of the Bible. Before we put it under the magnifying glass however, let us have a brief summary of it. The *New Bible Commentary* says of it:-

Here the author (John) states his purpose, and that (his) purpose (in writing his Gospel) is to in- culcate a specific kind of faith, that is, in the Mes- siahship and divine sonship of Jesus, which will lead to an inheritance of life in His name.

Dividing the verse into four, notice:-

1. The Sacred Book
2. The Saving Belief
3. The Superlative Being
4. The Supernatural Blessing

## 1. The Sacred Book

*These are <u>written</u> ...*

The Christian Faith is a religion of the Book. Its final authority, founding and grounding are written words on a page - the Holy Bible. The Bible is no less than God's Own revelation of Himself - God's very Own written Word. Christ, of course - as John points out - is God's Word in the flesh. He is the Word of God incarnate. But the living Word and the written Word are inextricable. If we would know Christ we must know the Bible - and the more acquainted we are with the Bible, the better acquainted we will get with the Christ of the Bible.

*These are written* ... written with a purpose, namely so that we might have eternal life through believing in the crucified, risen Saviour unfolded by John in his Gospel. The *Shorter Catechism* is pertinent here. It opens with the well known question and answer:-

Q. What is the chief end of man?

A. Man's chief end is to glorify God and to enjoy Him forever.

It then goes on:-

Q. What rule hath God given to direct us how we may glorify and enjoy Him?

A. The Word of God, which is contained in the Scriptures of the Old and New Testaments is the only rule to direct us how we may glorify and enjoy Him.

*These are <u>written</u> ...*

My heart is leaning on the Word
The written Word of God
Salvation by my Saviour's Name
Salvation through His blood.

## The Inspired Word

In 2 Timothy 3:16 we read *All Scripture is inspired by God ...* 'Inspired' here means 'God breathed.' Words are vocalised breath which express the thoughts of our minds. Scripture then is the product of divine breathing . Scripture is the result of the moving of God's Holy Spirit upon the minds and pens of the human authors of the Bible like John. This ensured that they wrote infallibly and inerrantly just what Almighty God wanted them to write. And this ensured that they wrote just what Almighty God would have us know concerning what we are to believe and how we are to behave if we are to have a happy life, a happy death and a happy eternity.

The 'Divine Inspiration of the Holy Scriptures' is one of the fundamental fundamentals of the Christian Faith, as all, in a sense, flows from this. On the divine inspiration of the Scriptures rests the Bible's truth, authority and power to save. Here is not ordinary book. Here is the Book of God and God of all books.

*These are written ... All Scripture is inspired by God.* The written words of John's Gospel, and the written words of the whole Bible are divinely inspired words. 'Inspiration' is a technical, Christian word. It refers to the special, supernatural work of the Holy Spirit in the lives of the writers of the Bible, enabling them to produce a trustworthy revelation of God Himself. God has revealed Himself in written words for us to read! The Holy Spirit of God has given to us a dependable, trustworthy revelation of God Himself and made known to us clearly God's Own way of salvation - His way of *eternal life.* The Bible then is no mere human book. It stands alone. *First of all you must understand this, that no prophecy of Scripture is a matter of one's own interpretation, because no prophecy ever came by the impulse of man, but men moved by the Holy Spirit spoke (wrote) from God* (2 Peter 1:20,21).

*These are written ...* The Sacred Book - the written Word of God. It is incumbent upon us to read and heed this Book. It is imperative that we believe this Book. It is essential that we know it, love it, treasure it, memorise it and proclaim its message of life to the lost world around us. *These are written.* The Sacred Book:-

How wonderful the Book divine
By inspiration given
Bright as a lamp its doctrines shine
To guide our souls to heaven

Its light, descending from above
Our sin-sick world to cheer
Displays a Saviour's boundless grace
And brings His glories near

It shows to man his wandering feet
And where his feet have trod
And brings to view the matchless grace
Of our forgiving God

It lights our path, it lifts our hearts
Along the upward way
It life and joy and peace imparts
Till dawns eternal day.

## 2. The Saving Belief

*These are written that you may <u>believe</u> that Jesus is the Christ, the Son of God, and that by <u>believing</u> you may have life in His name* (John 20:31).

The New Testament in general, and John's Gospel here in particular, are both adamant that salvation - having eternal life - is gained by believing, and not by doing or working. John's most famous verse, sometimes referred to as 'the gospel in a nutshell' reads: *God so loved the world that He gave His only Son, that whoever <u>believes</u> in Him should not perish but have eternal life.* John

47

3:36 states *He who <u>believes</u> in the Son has eternal life.* And the Lord Jesus, in John 5:24 affirmed: *'Truly, truly, I say to you, he who hears My word and <u>believes</u> Him Who sent Me has eternal life; he does not come into judgment but has passed from death to life.'*

The Saving Belief. In the Bible, receiving Christ as one's own, personal Saviour, trusting Him for full salvation and believing in Him amount to the same thing. Believing in Him, trusting Him and having faith in Him are synonyms. *But to all who received Him, who believed in His name, He gave power to become children of God* (John 1:12).

What then does it mean to believe in Jesus? What exactly does it mean to have saving faith in Him? The *Shorter Catechism's* definition of saving faith is unsurpassed:-

Q. What is faith in Jesus Christ?

A. Faith in Jesus Christ is a saving grace, where-by we receive and rest upon Him alone for salva-tion, as He is offered to us in the Gospel.

Believing in Jesus means trusting - or entrusting - our souls to Him as our Saviour. We rest on Him and His work at Calvary alone for our salvation, and not in anything we are or we may or can do to supposedly earn God's favour. Our plea is 'Christ only.' The Gospel exhortation which we proclaim to a lost world is *Believe in the Lord Jesus and you will be saved* (Acts 16:31).

The Bible is clear that salvation is by believing, not by do-ing. This is so because salvation is by God's grace and not by hu-man works. *By grace you have been saved through faith, and this is not your own doing, it is the gift of God, not because of works lest any man should boast* (Ephesians 2:8,9). God's grace can only be received by faith. Faith is the empty hand which reaches out and receives the grace of God in Christ on the cross with gratitude.

The blessing of eternal life then - a synonym for salvation - is a matter of the gift of God, not the graft of man. That eternal life is gained by believing is the touchstone and distinguishing mark of Biblical Christianity. It is this which separates the Christian Faith from all the other faiths of the world. All other religions and faiths view eternal life as something which we do and earn. It is a reward for our goodness. The Christian however, acknowledging his/her sin, looks to Christ's righteousness for salvation, and nothing or no one else. The Christian Faith proclaims that eternal life is gained solely by believing in the crucified Christ Who died to save sinners - Who died to give us eternal life:-

<blockquote>
Not saved are we by trying<br>
From self can come no aid<br>
Tis on the blood relying<br>
Once for our ransom paid<br>
Tis looking unto Jesus<br>
The Holy One and Just<br>
Tis His great work that saves us<br>
It is not try but trust<br>
<br>
No deeds of ours are needed<br>
To make Christ's merit more<br>
No frames of mind or feelings<br>
Can add to His great store<br>
Tis simply to receive Him<br>
The Holy One and Just<br>
Tis only to believe Him -<br>
It is not try but trust.
</blockquote>

The saving belief. Salvation/eternal life is by believing. Faith though has an object - there can be misplaced faith. The object of the Christian's saving faith is not a creed, but a Person - an incomparable Person. And this brings us to our third point. Our faith is in:-

## 3. The Superlative Being

*These are written that you may believe that <u>Jesus</u> is the Christ, the Son of God ...*

Under God then, John wrote his Gospel to direct our minds, hearts and faith to Jesus. 'Jesus' is the human name given to the Saviour. His title though is *the Christ* - that is, the 'anointed one' or Messiah. And His identity is absolutely staggering. He is no less than the unique *Son of God*, says John. We come then to the Superlative Being - the Person of the Lord Jesus Christ. Christianity is Christ. Its centre and focus is on a specific Person - an incomparable Person - delineated here as *Jesus ... the Christ, the Son of God.*

### i. *Jesus is the Christ*

'Christ' is a title. It means 'the anointed one' or 'Messiah.' In Old Testament times prophets, priests and kings were anointed. It signified their being set apart by God and especially endowed with the Holy Spirit so they could fulfil the particular role and sphere of service appointed to them. The Jews though longed for the coming of *the* Anointed One - the Messiah promised by God, Who would come to redeem His people. In the Lord Jesus the Messiah came, and the promises of God were wonderfully fulfilled. He is the Christ. Peter confessed to Him *'You are the Christ, the Son of the living God'* (Matthew 16:16).

Did the Lord Jesus Himself believe Himself to be the Christ/Messiah though? Or was His messiah-hood projected onto Him by the church? John's Gospel shows that Jesus did believe Himself to be the Messiah. John 4:25 ff. *The woman (of Samaria) said to Him 'I know that Messiah is coming (He Who is called Christ); when He comes, He will show us all things. Jesus said to her, ' I Who speak to you am He.'* So *Jesus is the Christ* - the Anointed One. James Montgomery wrote apt lines when he wrote:-

Hail to the Lord's Anointed

Great David's Greater Son

Hail, in the time appointed

His reign on earth begun

He comes to break oppression

To set the captive free

To take away transgression

And rule in equity.


But John says more. John would have us believe that Jesus is the Christ, but He would also have us believe in His deity - that Jesus Christ is God: the Son of God and God the Son.


ii. *Jesus is ... the Son of God*

Christianity is Christ, and Jesus Christ is God - the Son of God and God the Son, the second Person of the ever blessed Trinity. The absolute deity of Christ is one of the basic fundamentals of the Christian Faith. If we deny that Jesus is God, we cannot claim to be Christian. If we open John's Gospel anywhere, we will find the deity of Christ somewhere. The divine son-ship of Christ is part of John's Gospel's very warp and woof:-

John's Gospel reaches a climax with Thomas confessing to the risen Christ '*My Lord and my God*' (John 20:28). It is noticeable that Christ did not rebuke Thomas for idolatry. John's Gospel opens with the statement *In the beginning was the Word, and the Word was with God, and the Word was God* (John 1:1). John's Gospel records the deeds of Jesus. He performed many miracles - signs - which only One who is God can do. Jesus turned water into wine (John 2); Jesus healed a paralysed man (John 5); Jesus fed a crowd of five thousand plus with just five loaves and two fish (John 6); Jesus gave sight to a man blind from birth (John 9); Jesus raised Lazarus from the dead (John 11). His works betray Him. He is *the Son of God.*

The words of Jesus betray Him also. He used the divine name - the I AM WHO I AM of Exodus 3:14 - and applied it to Himself. For example *'I am the light of the world'* (John 8:12); *'I am the Good Shepherd'* (John 10:11); *'I am the resurrection and the life'* (John 11:25); *'I am the way and the truth and the life'* (John 14:6). Truly, no one ever spoke like this Man. He was either deluded or divine. Mad or the Messiah. A lunatic, liar or Lord of all. Christians believe - on the unadorned biblical evidence - that Jesus is the Son of God and God the Son. His works and words, actions and announcements, conduct and conversation were such that no other conclusion can be drawn. And the Person and Work of Christ cannot be separated. It is because He is Who His is that Jesus can do what He does - bestow eternal life. He is God. He is incomparable in His being and incomparable in His blessing. He alone can save. He alone can impart eternal salvation to our souls. He alone can bestow the gift of eternal life. Glory to His name! He is the Son of God. Hence He is ever to be worshipped and adored.

Join all the glorious names

Of wisdom love and power

That mortals ever knew

That angels ever bore

All are too mean to speak His worth

Too mean to set my Saviour forth.

Finally, from John's key verse, we note:-

## 4. The Supernatural Blessing

...*Life in His name.* The supernatural blessing is *life* - by which John means 'eternal life.' Eternal life is the greatest blessing we can ever or will ever receive. It cannot be bettered or improved upon. It is a supernatural blessing because this world cannot give us eternal life. It cannot be bought. Thankfully, this world is unable to take this blessing of all blessings away from us either, for the Bible assures us that nothing can ever separate God's children from the love of God in Christ Jesus our Lord.

John wrote His Gospel then so that we might have/experience/enjoy something - something wonderful beyond compare. *These are written that you might believe that Jesus is the Christ, the Son of God, and that believing you may have life in His name* (John 20:31). In John 3:36 we read *He who believes in the son has eternal life.* Jesus Himself said in John 10:10 *'I came that they may have life and have it abundantly.'*

## New Life in Christ

The Bible's diagnosis of us is that by nature we are spiritually dead - *dead through the trespasses and sins in which you once walked* (Ephesians 2:1). Our sinful condition makes us dead to God, and separates us from Him. But Jesus came to give us life. Paradoxically, Jesus died to give us life. He died that our sins might be forgiven and so be reconciled to God and enjoy His friendship and fellowship for time and eternity. Fellowship with God is the life we were made for - Life indeed. The Bible is adamant that Jesus, and Jesus alone is able to impart this supernal, supernatural and superlative gift of eternal life to dead sinners. *For the wages of sin is death but the free gift of God is eternal life in Christ Jesus our Lord* (Romans 6:23). Eternal life is the supreme blessing. In John 17:3 Jesus defined this supreme blessing so: *'This is eternal life that they know Thee the only true God and Jesus Christ whom Thou hast sent.'*

The *Lion Concise Bible Encyclopedia* has the following pertinent comment under the heading 'Life':-

> There is more to life than just physical existence. A relationship with God enables people to live life on a new level. This is the full, abundant life that Jesus came to bring. It is 'eternal life', which Jesus offers as a free and permanent gift. Eternal life is life in a new dimension, 'God's life.' 'Whoever has the Son' says John, 'has this life.' It begins when a person becomes a Christian, and survives death. It is an eternal relationship with God.

Our chief end as human beings made in the image of God is to 'glorify God and to enjoy Him forever.' And it is Jesus alone Who enables us to realise this, our chief end. Life without Jesus borders on a contradiction in terms. He alone is the one mediator between God and man. His death alone is the only means by which our sins may be forgiven and we have peace with God. He alone, as the Son of God and God the Son, is able to bestow on us the greatest gift of all - the gift of eternal life. Note that John delineates this life as *life in His Name.* That is, life by all Who Jesus is and life by virtue of all that He has done on the cross of Calvary to save sinners. John would have us believe in Jesus and so know life indeed - the very life of God experienced today, a quality of life beyond compare.

So we have been considering the golden key to John's Gospel - the Gospel of the divine Son of God and Gospel of eternal life. *These are written so that you might believe that Jesus is the Christ the Son of God and that believing you may have life in His name.* This key verse draws our attention to a Sacred Book, Saving Belief, Superlative Being and Supernatural Blessing. John would have us know and rejoice in Jesus: the life-giving and eternal life bestowing Saviour and Son of God:-

Life, life, eternal life!

Jesus alone is the Giver

Life, life, abundant life

Glory to Jesus forever!